A Gift called Shane

by

Ricky Watters

illustrated by

Penny Weber

Soro Publishing

This book is dedicated to all my fellow adoptees.
Stay true to yourself, and don't be afraid to shine.

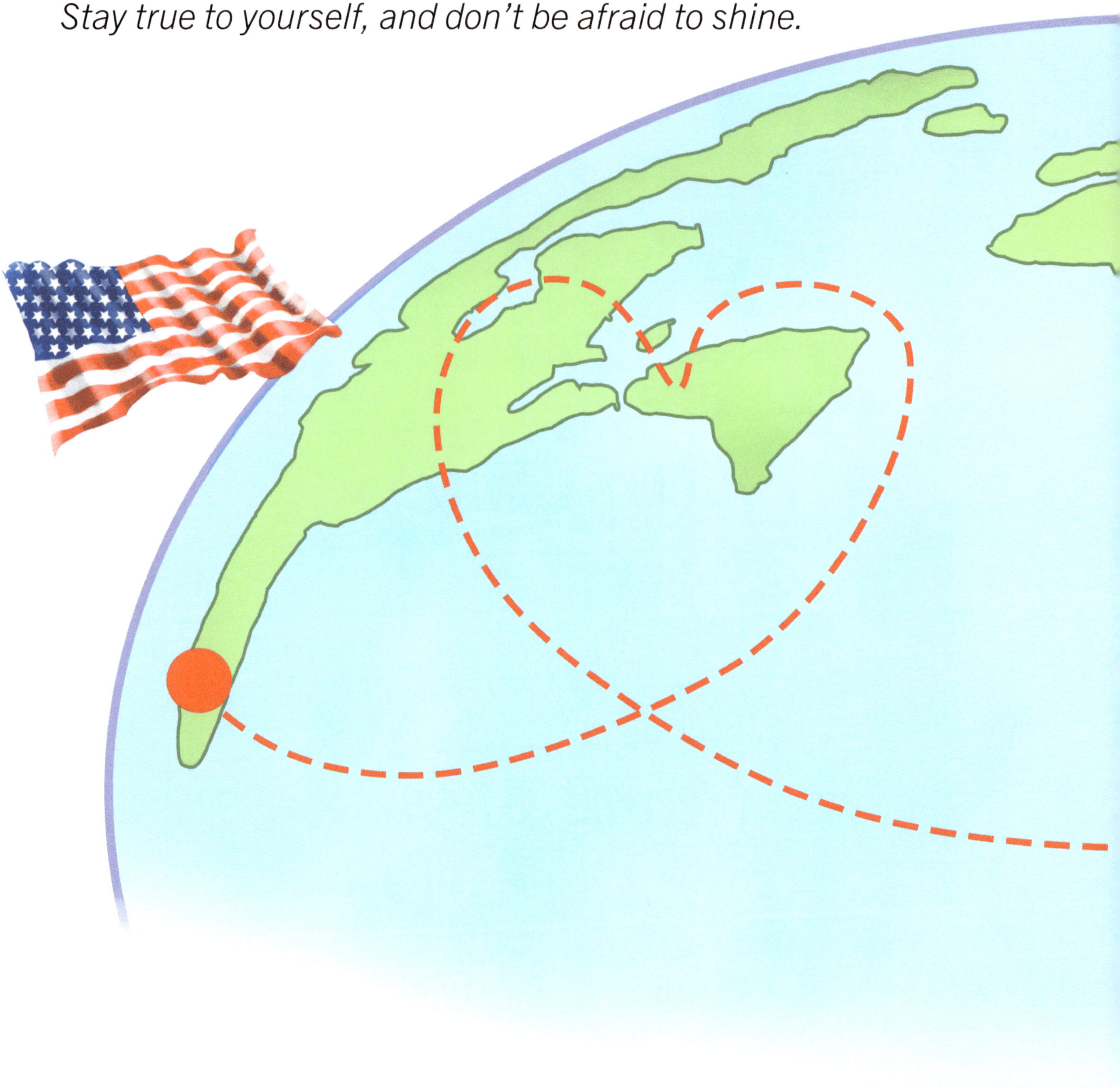

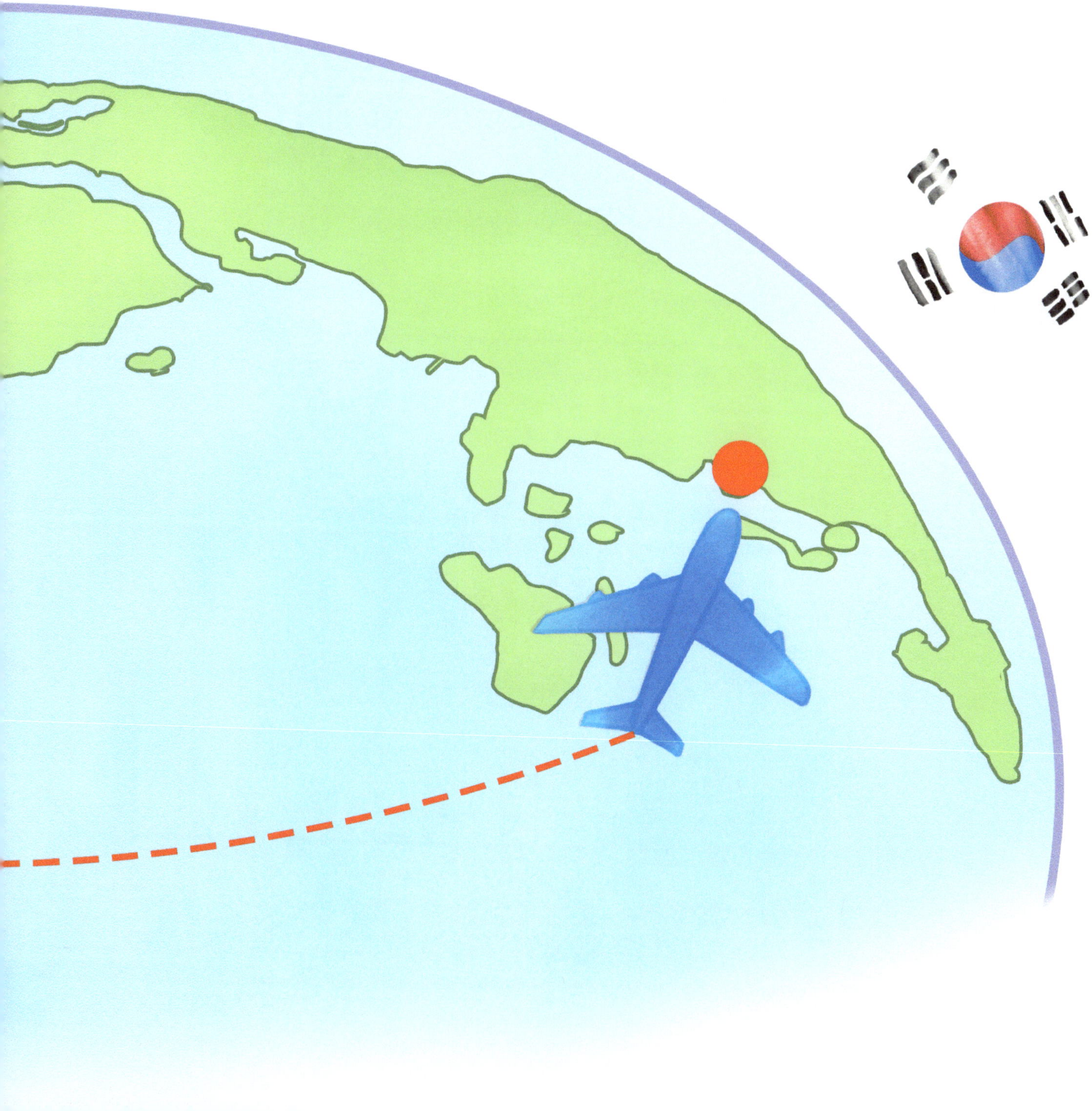

It seemed to be another day,
much like all the others.
The sun was beginning to fade,
as I went in the house for supper.

As I sat down at the table to eat,
I noticed a plate at the empty seat.

The tearful sparkle in Mom's eyes
couldn't hide the big surprise.

32
RACECAR
3
RACECAR

My prayers were answered.
My dream came true.
I now have a little brother
to come home to!

Mom always said there were kids who felt alone,
who needed love and comfort from a real family home.
God knew from the start our paths would meet,
and our lives would finally be complete.

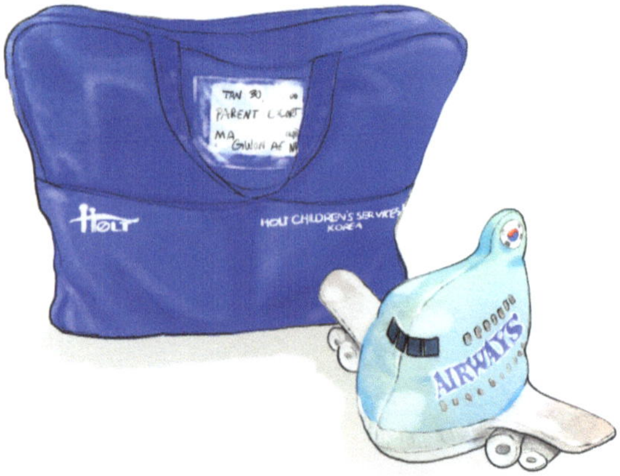

We brought our Gift home
from overseas.

He cried all the way;
nothing put him at ease.

Not even a hug from his cuddly teddy bear
made him aware of how much we cared.

But the moment he entered our happy home
he must have felt no longer alone.
He was no longer surrounded by strangers,
and he was clearly not in any danger.

He seemed to calm right down
as we gave him a chance to look around.

At all the warm, smiling faces
of the new family he had found.

Mom and Dad were eager to explain;
God had given us more than money and fame.
I promised to protect him and never complain.
I'll forever remind him we're one and the same.

He needed a Mom and a Dad
and a really Big Brother
To guide him through all the wonders
he would soon discover.

Where there once was three,
now there's four.

Where there once was a void,
now there's laughter and joy.

I’ll stay by his side at all times.
A friend in me he can always confide.
Makes no difference I’m only nine.
I’ll make sure he has the tools to shine.

He is my little brother;
that will never change.
No matter how he came,
I will love him just the same.

Of all the great things I've achieved
nothing could replace the love I received…

From a gift called Shane.

The End

ISBN 978-1-965438-00-8
Library of Congress Control Number: 2024918845

For more information about the author, please visit www.rickywatters.com.

Published by Soro Publishing
For more information about our books and authors, visit our website: www.soropublishing.com.

Milton Keynes UK
Ingram Content Group UK Ltd.
UKHW050046301024
450402UK00009B/88